STORIEZ

A Group Treatment Guide

by Dr. Meagan Corrado

Acknowledgments

Dr. Meagan acknowledges and wholeheartedly thanks:

- The youth and clinicians whose group experiences inspired the creation of this book
- Dr. Christine Courtois and Professor Thomas Hurtser for their meaningful feedback in the development of this resource
- Jeremy Guay, graphic designer and owner of Peregrine Creative
- Leon Rainbow, graffiti artist and Storiez logo creator
- The children, teenagers, and adults who contributed to this project through participation in photos and videography

Copyright © 2018 by Dr. Meagan Corrado

All rights reserved. No part of this publication may be reproduced, stored in a retrieval system, or transmitted, in any form or by any means, electronic, mechanical, photocopying, recording, or otherwise without the prior permission of the author.

Printed in the United States of America

First Printing, 2018

ISBN: 978-1-7325813-0-2

Printed by Ingram Spark

www.ingramspark.com

Table of Contents

Introduction

There is no fool-proof way to facilitate a successful group. There is no formula. There are no short-cuts, magical potions, or secret recipes. Every group is different. Some groups are quiet and passive. Other groups are overly activated. Group dynamics change from one session to the next. Alliances and connections forged during one session may morph into adversarial chaos in the next. Group priorities and goals change.

"How do you implement the Storiez trauma narrative intervention in a group," clinicians and community leaders have asked me. I often smile and pause for a moment. I pause not because I am reaching for an answer. I pause because I know that my answer cannot be crammed into a ten minute question and answer session at the end of a training. The question is loaded. There are too many factors, too many variables in groups for me to provide one cookie-cutter answer.

As I reflect on this question- a question asked of me many times by clinicians working in a variety of settings- I find myself going back to the beginning. My graduate social work education at Bryn Mawr College. I took an elective course called "Group Treatment," taught by Professor Thomas Hurster. In the class, which included our own experiential group, we learned about the therapeutic factors of groups. Their developmental stages. The benefits, pitfalls, and challenges of groups. I developed a deep appreciation and respect for the chaos and possibility inherent in group treatment.

Upon graduating, I found myself thrown into group facilitation in a variety of settings- from schools to summer camps to residential treatment facilities. They looked and felt different than the classroom-based group in Professor Hurtser's class. Yet they also felt strangely familiar. I loved them. I loved their chaos and their possibility. Their destructiveness and their creativity.

As I continued my role as a group (and individual) clinician in a variety of settings, I had conversations with colleagues. Conversations about the impossible task we were charged with- creating healthy, functioning groups in the context of random, chaotic settings. Many of my colleagues were frustrated. Under-prepared. Overwhelmed. Burnt out.

As I reflect on my own social work education, I value the instrumental role that Professor Hurster's group treatment course has had in my own practice. But I also feel empathy for those colleagues who never had the opportunity to learn about group treatment. Many were thrown into a tsunami and expected to swim.

This resource seeks to fill a need- a need for deeper knowledge about the group treatment process. A need for skills in building and maintaining healthy groups. A need for guidance regarding how to facilitate the creation of trauma narratives in a group setting.

Group treatment is DYNAMIC and COMPLEX .

The Complexity of Groups: Strengths and Challenges

The complexity of group treatment cannot be undermined. Groups contain the seeds of transformation and change. They also hold the potential for chaos, conflict, and destruction. When facilitating groups, it is important to acknowledge the curative, therapeutic effects of group treatment as well as the presence of destructive forces. Reflection on the developmental stages of groups also provides meaningful insight into the group process.

The Therapeutic Power of the Group

Group treatment has incredible potential to facilitate therapeutic growth and healing. There are a variety of factors that make groups valuable. Groups enable individuals to experiment with new roles, gain new perspectives on current and past challenges, and develop new patterns in relationships. They provide members with the opportunity to connect with others. The group itself can serve as a source of hope and inspiration. Mackenzie (as cited in Brabender, Fallon, & Smolar) identifies four categories of therapeutic factors in groups: supportive factors, self-revelation, learning from others, and psychological work (2004, p 86-101). Yalom (1970) speaks to the power of the group as an "agent of change" (p. 120). Nitsun (1996) states that groups are an opportunity for transformative play in which members can experiment with alternative solutions to problems (p. 213).

Group treatment is therapeutically valuable for trauma survivors. Groups can serve as a safe space for traumatized individuals to collectively process past experiences and make sense of their present and future. Phillips (2013) states of the therapeutic potential of trauma groups, "[Group] affords safety, allows remembering and mourning, and facilitates reconnection in and through an intersubjective context with others" (p. 32). Groups support trauma survivors in experiencing an increased sense of control and also provide members with the opportunity to play the dual roles of both "victim and helper" (Van der Kolk, 1987, p. 163). Group treatment offers an opportunity for healthy reconnection in the face of fragmentation and dissociation (Johnson, 1987, p. 12). Judith Herman (as cited in Phillips, 2013) adds, "The solidarity of a group provides the strongest protection against terror and despair, and the strongest antidote to traumatic experience" (p. 37).

Creativity, Destruction, and Chaos in Groups

While there are multiple factors that point to the therapeutic value of groups, there are also challenges within the group context. Bringing individuals with psychological and interpersonal difficulties together in the same room at the same time can seem like a daunting task (Nitsun, 1996). There are many challenges that group facilitators and members face. Nitsun (1996) coined the term the "anti-group" to describe "the destructive aspects of groups that threaten the integrity of the group and its therapeutic development" (p. 44). The anti-group takes many different forms and can rear its destructive head through a wide range of "attitudes and impulses, conscious and unconscious" (Nitsun, 1996, p. 44). From silence and passive aggression to explosivity and blaming, each of these anti-group behaviors threaten the health and development of the group (Haen & Weil, 2010; Nitsun, 1996).

In the face of anti-group behaviors, clinicians often panic or freeze. But Nitsun suggests that the successful group facilitator should both acknowledge the existence of the anti-group and seek to harness the potential of the anti-group to facilitate creative growth and progress. Winnicott (2005) introduced the term "creative destruction." He proposed that creativity cannot occur without some form of destruction. Building on this concept, Nitsun states that in order for deep change and growth to occur, both the creative and destructive forces of a group must be harnessed, exploited, and given space. Destruction in the group is necessary in order to build confidence, cohesion, and growth. It is necessary for depth and change. Nitsun suggests that "the threatened destructive 'collapse' may contain the seeds of survival and growth, generating and regenerating the constructive potential of the group" (1996, p. 208). The anti-group is not the enemy to productive group processing and therapeutic group interaction; it is one of the necessary components for a robust, dynamic group, "The anti-group forms an essential part of the dialectic of creative and destructive forces in group psychotherapy, that it is in the movement between the two poles that the group develops, and that it is in the opposition of thesis and antithesis that a new synthesis, a transformation may take place" (Nitsun, 1996, p. 197).

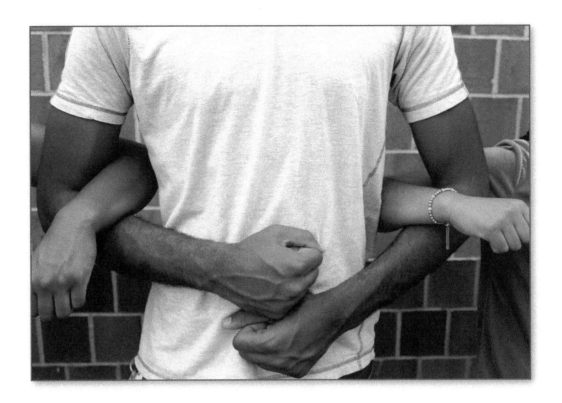

In a similar vein, Haen & Weil (2010) speak to the chaos that often occurs in group contexts. They suggest that the effective group facilitator must learn how to "work at the edge of chaos" (p. 43). They state that there must be an attitude of openness, acceptance, and respect when chaos ensues, "Embrace the chaos that the teenagers carry around with them and that they bring into group...Rather than trying to clamp it down or squeeze it into a box, we instead attempt to transform the energy that fuels the chaos by channeling it into action in the service of treatment" (Haen & Weil, 2010, p. 44). Working at the edge of chaos requires the group leader to embrace it with confidence, knowing that after the group has conquered the chaos, then growth, healing, and connection can occur (Haen & Weil, 2010, p. 49). Nitsun (as cited by Haen & Weil, 2010) creates a meaningful parallel between a creator's artistic process and a leader's facilitation of group treatment:

I believe that art is meaningless without some confrontation with the dark side; similarly, that the group experience is incomplete and likely to be superficial without such recognition. Holding together the constructive and the destructive potential is a major requirement of the group therapist, as I believe it is in the artistic process...Sometimes the tension between the two is very great, even unbearable, but usually there comes a point of reconciliation, of synthesis, and a new form emerges...Eventually an understanding, an insight, a change is achieved. (p. 49)

Group Developmental Stages

Sensorimotor, preoperational, concrete, and formal. Trust versus mistrust. Autonomy versus shame and doubt. The contributions of Piaget and Erikson provide us with insight into the typical developmental tasks of an individual at an identified stage. These stages educate us on the challenges and triumphs that are typical for individuals progressing through each stage. They provide emotional, social, and cognitive landmarks that serve as a guide for healthy development. These stages also assist others in managing expectations for the individual based on his/her cognitive, emotional, and interpersonal capabilities. In groups, not only are members progressing developmentally as individuals, but the group as a whole also progresses through developmental stages.

Tuckman (1965) proposes a developmental model of groups. He suggests that groups simultaneously progress through two sets of developmental stages. The first set of developmental stages relate to the social interactions within the group. These steps answer the question, "How will group members interact with one another at different points in the group's process?" Step one is "testing and dependence." Group members discover and explore the boundaries of the group and learn the norms and expectations for group interaction. Step two, "intragroup conflict," is characterized by resistance and hostility. The group resists its "groupness," and members seek to assert their individuality. In step three, "development of group cohesion," the group accepts boundaries and norms and develops a collective sense of "we." During the fourth step, "functional role-relatedness," individuals begin to use the group as a tool for problem solving. They experiment with different roles and solutions.

The second set of developmental stages (Tuckman, 1965) relate to the group's ability to achieve its overall task or goal. These stages answer the question, "What will the group do as it works toward its goal?" Step one is "orientation to the task." Individuals learn how the group will assist them in achieving an identified goal. Step two, "emotional response to task demands," involves resistance to the group task. The individual's needs over-ride the group's commitment to its collective goal. In step three, "open exchange of relevant interpretations," individual group members share their perspectives as they work toward the overall goal. During step four, "emergence of solutions," the group collectively works to fully realize its task.

For a clear developmental picture of the tasks the group will undertake and the manner in which they will interact, the clinician must consider how each of these parallel processes merge. Tuckman (1965) summarizes the integration of the social and task-oriented stages as follows: (1) forming, (2) storming, (3) norming, and (4) performing. He suggests that groups progress through these developmental stages as they seek to achieve interpersonal and task-related goals. Later in his career, Tuckman added a 5th stage, "adjourning" to capture the group experience of separation and termination (Bonebright, 2010).

Understanding the developmental stages of groups assists the group facilitator in making realistic expectations for the group given its developmental "age." This knowledge normalizes social and task-related challenges and successes. Further, it provides the group facilitator with a framework for understanding the group's limitations and possibilities.

Tuckman's Stages of Group Development

	(1) **Testing and dependence**	(2) **Intragroup conflict**	(3) **Development of group cohesion**	(4) **Functional role-relatedness**
How will group members interact with one another at different points in the group's process?	• Members discover and explore the boundaries of the group • Members learn the norms and expectations for group interaction	• Resistance and hostility • Group resists its "groupness" • Members seek to assert their individuality	• Group accepts boundaries and norms • Group develops a collective sense of "we"	• Individuals begin to use the group as a tool for problem solving • Members experiment with different roles and solutions

⊕   ⊕   ⊕   ⊕

	(1) **Orientation to the task**	(2) **Emotional response to task demands**	(3) **Open exchange of relevant interpretations**	(4) **Emergence of solutions**
What will the group do as it works toward its goal?	• Individuals learn how the group will assist them in achieving an identified goal	• Resistance to the group task • Individual's needs over-ride the group's commitment to its collective goal	• Individual group members share their perspectives as they work toward the overall goal	• Group collectively works to fully realize its task

⊜   ⊜   ⊜   ⊜

FORMING	**STORMING**	**NORMING**	**PERFORMING**

Information derived from Tuckman's (1965) developmental model of groups.

Every group has its own unique STRENGTHS and CHALLENGES.

Defining the Group

A group is a collection of individuals unified by a goal, purpose, task, or vision. There are a variety of group types. Groups can be closed or open. Psychoeducational or exploratory. Thematic or process-oriented. Time limited or ongoing. The group type chosen by the facilitator should be informed by the needs of the individuals in the group and the setting in which the group is being provided. Careful assessment of contextual and treatment factors are essential when determining the type of group being facilitated.

Group composition

Composition supports the facilitator in determining who to include in a group and who to exclude. Group composition is not an exercise in judgment or exclusivity. It is an important step in developing a balanced group that facilitates safety, progress, and growth. Factors to consider when composing a group is the total number of group members, homogeneity and heterogeneity, and inclusion/exclusion criteria.

The ideal number of group members is 6 to 8 for an adolescent group and 6 to 10 for an adult group (Hurtser, 2009). Consideration of the total number of group members is important. If the group is too small, it cannot benefit from the diversity of individual personalities, perspectives, and challenges. If a group is too large, there is an increased likelihood for the development of subgroups or "cliques," skewed participation, competition for leadership, and the ability to hide treatment behaviors (Hurster, 2009).

Achieving a balance between heterogeneity and homogeneity is another important element of group composition. Heterogeneity refers to the differences between individuals. Homogeneity are those qualities that individuals share. Yalom (1970) suggests that healthy group composition should seek to achieve "maximum heterogeneity in the client's conflict areas and patterns of coping, and at the same time strive for homogeneity of the clients' degree of vulnerability and capacity to tolerate anxiety" (p. 272-273). Brabender, Fallon, & Smolar (2004) propose that each individual in a group should have someone with whom they can potentially connect based on personal characteristics, challenges, or experiences (p. 65). Kahn & Aronson (2007) propose that for trauma groups, clinicians should "look for a thread of commonality in the trauma" (p. 286).

Group facilitators must determine the degree to which homogeneity and heterogeneity are important to the specific goals of the group being facilitated. Yalom (1970) speaks to the advantages and disadvantages of homogeneity and heterogeneity in group composition, "Homogeneous groups jell more quickly, become more cohesive, offer more immediate support to group members, are better attended, have less conflict, and provide more rapid relief of symptoms," however heterogeneous groups are able to achieve more depth and pronounced transformation in the face of "dissonance or incongruity" (p. 272-273). The group clinician must achieve a delicate balance between sameness and difference.

Which clients are appropriate for group and which clients are not yet ready? There are multiple factors that should inform clinicians' decisions regarding whether or not a client is "group ready." The literature suggests that individuals who are anxious about participation but intrigued by the possibilities are ideal candidates for group. Motivation for participation is an essential factor in group readiness (Yalom, 1970, p. 248). Group members' goals for participation must align with the overall vision/goal of the group (Yalom, 1970). Consideration of the following questions is also important: (1) Is the group an appropriate setting for the individual and (2) Can the individual offer the group something? (Brabender, Fallon, & Smolar, 2004). The group facilitator must also consider whether or not an individual's symptoms or behaviors could be potentially toxic if displayed in a group setting. If symptoms or behaviors are potentially hazardous to the health of the group, other treatment modalities may be a better fit for that particular individual.

Pre-Group Interviews

Before bringing members of a group together for the first session, it is beneficial to conduct pre-group interviews with each potential member. Pre-group interviews allow the clinician to obtain useful information about the individual's strengths, challenges, personal qualities, and attitude toward group treatment. The interview also provides the facilitator with the opportunity to clarify the goal and structure of the group, solidify group boundaries and norms, and answer relevant questions. The information obtained during a pre-group interview provides useful information when determining group composition, individual and group readiness, session structure, and potential topics/themes. Every clinician may not have the luxury of flexibility as it relates to group composition. Pre-group interviews are still beneficial to set the stage for the group and to plan for potential challenges and opportunities.

Pre-Group Interview

Name _____ Date _____ Age _____

Hi, my name is (introduce self). I am meeting with everyone who is interested in group (or who has been chosen for group) to see if it will be a good fit for them. This group will meet every (frequency) on (day of the week). There will be other (kids/teenagers/adults) in this group who will be participating as well. We will be working on (theme) and creating our stories. I'm going to ask you some questions to learn more about you. If you have any questions as we talk, please feel free to ask.

1. Have you ever participated in a group?

   _____

2. What was helpful about it?

   _____

3. What was challenging?

   _____

4. How do you feel about participating in this group?

   _____

5. What are your strengths as a person?

   _____

6. Name a few things about yourself that you would like to work on.

   _____

7. How can participating in a group help you?

   _____

8. What could you contribute to a group?

   _____

9. Is there any additional information about you that would be helpful for me to know?

   _____

   _____

Within the context of a healthy group, individuals can *HEAL* and *GROW*.

Choosing a Theoretical Group Approach

Clinicians providing individual therapy must determine a theoretical lens from which to interpret and approach a client's challenges. The theoretical approach guides a practitioner's interactions with their clients. Group leaders must identify which theoretical approach they will implement in a group context. Braender, Fallon, & Smolar (2004) identify seven potential theoretical models for group facilitators to employ: interpersonal, psychodynamic, social systems, cognitive behavioral, psychodrama, redecision, and existential. Summarized here are five of the approaches commonly implemented in group settings (Brabender, Fallon, & Smolar, 2004)*:

Interpersonal	Our desire for connection with others drives our behavior. The group is viewed as a mini world or a "microcosm" of the real world. It serves as an opportunity for individuals to develop healthier connections and experiment with new roles. If group members can improve connections and successfully adopt new roles in the group, they can apply the same knowledge and skills to outside relationships.
Psychodynamic	Everything that we do happens for a reason- whether conscious or unconscious. If we look deeply into the function of our behavior, we can uncover meaning. The group is a means to revealing unconscious motivations with the goal of helping people come to a deeper understanding of themselves.
Social Systems	Systems are complex. Every system is interconnected. Systems mutually influence one another through the transmission of information. The group is a system, and each individual in a group is influenced by his/her own subsystems. Group interactions allow for transmission of information. This exchange of information then influences the group, the individual, and the individual's subsystems.
Cognitive-Behavioral	Individuals experience challenges because of unhealthy thinking. Unhealthy thinking leads to distressing symptoms. The group supports individuals in reducing symptoms by developing healthy thoughts. This is achieved through psychoeducation and skill building.
Psychodrama	Our behavior influences our emotions and our thoughts. If we can change the way that we behave, we can change the way that we feel and think. The group provides members with the opportunity to recreate challenges through dramatic reenactments. During the reenactments, group members can experiment with alternative options for managing situations. This change in behavior will lead to changes in feelings and thoughts.

*Using a few sentences to summarize each of these group approaches minimizes the complexity of each model. This condensed information should be a springboard to deeper research and exploration as practitioners choose which models fit their client needs, clinical preference, and the demands of managed care, mental health agencies, and host settings.

Successful groups TRANSFORM chaos into CREATIVITY.

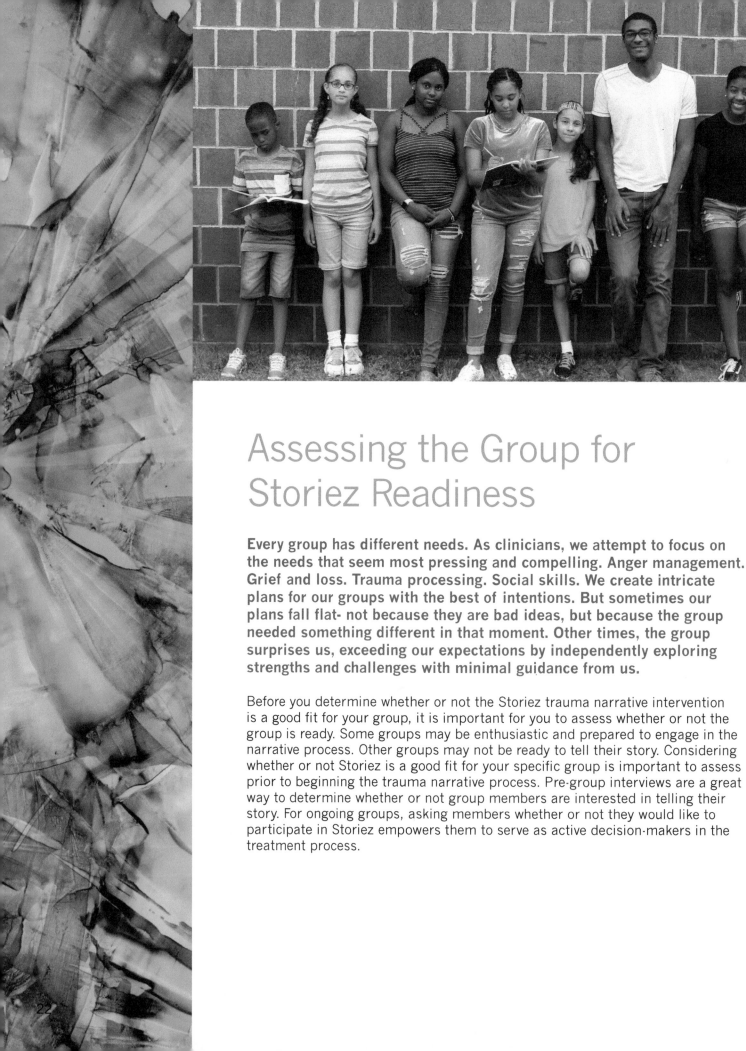

Assessing the Group for Storiez Readiness

Every group has different needs. As clinicians, we attempt to focus on the needs that seem most pressing and compelling. Anger management. Grief and loss. Trauma processing. Social skills. We create intricate plans for our groups with the best of intentions. But sometimes our plans fall flat- not because they are bad ideas, but because the group needed something different in that moment. Other times, the group surprises us, exceeding our expectations by independently exploring strengths and challenges with minimal guidance from us.

Before you determine whether or not the Storiez trauma narrative intervention is a good fit for your group, it is important for you to assess whether or not the group is ready. Some groups may be enthusiastic and prepared to engage in the narrative process. Other groups may not be ready to tell their story. Considering whether or not Storiez is a good fit for your specific group is important to assess prior to beginning the trauma narrative process. Pre-group interviews are a great way to determine whether or not group members are interested in telling their story. For ongoing groups, asking members whether or not they would like to participate in Storiez empowers them to serve as active decision-makers in the treatment process.

Evaluating the context in which you are providing group treatment is an important step in assessing group readiness for Storiez. Every context has strengths and challenges which may provide additional support in implementing Storiez or create barriers to healthy narrative processing. Each setting determines how long children/adolescents/adults will be admitted to the program, the scope of group treatment, and the length of sessions. Some settings lend themselves well to implementation of Storiez because they allow for consistent meeting times with a consistent group of participants. Other settings are particularly chaotic, and it is difficult to prepare for sessions. If groups are being provided in a host setting, the facilitator also has to consider the impact of emotions/thoughts incited in group on the individual's ability to reintegrate back into the host setting (e.g. schools, correctional facilities). Just because a particular setting has barriers does not mean that it would be harmful to implement Storiez in that context; it simply means that the group facilitator must be intentional, mindful, and creative about implementation.

Remember, Storiez is a guide that requires each practitioner to use their professional judgment and clinical skills when implementing. It is also a flexible tool that can meet the needs of a variety of populations with a variety of presenting challenges. Every Storiez process looks and feels different. Perhaps instead of having group members work on their entire life story, it may be more appropriate for them to work on a particular facet of their story (i.e. grief, anger, incarceration, substance abuse, school, adoption, foster care, etc.). If an entire group is processing the same trauma (a school shooting, the loss of a classmate, a natural disaster), it may be therapeutic for them to develop a collective group story. Remember, the Storiez steps are a guide. It is up to the group facilitator and the individuals/groups they are working with to determine what story format is conducive to the needs of the group.

When group members feel *SAFE*, they are able to connect, engage, and reflect.

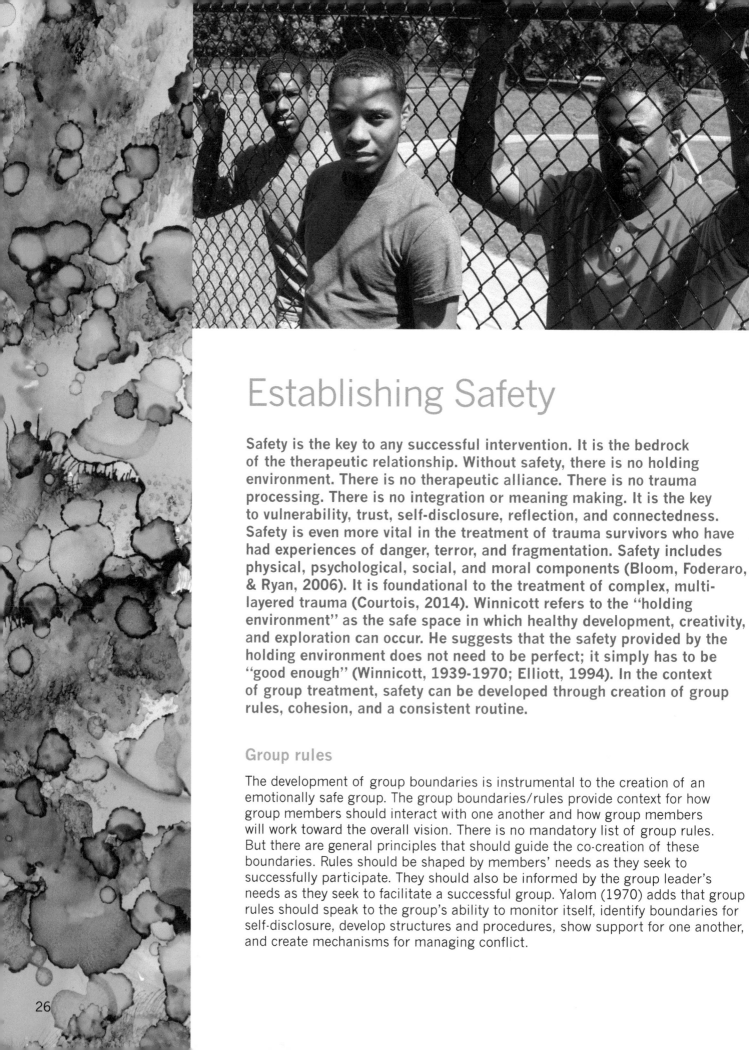

Establishing Safety

Safety is the key to any successful intervention. It is the bedrock of the therapeutic relationship. Without safety, there is no holding environment. There is no therapeutic alliance. There is no trauma processing. There is no integration or meaning making. It is the key to vulnerability, trust, self-disclosure, reflection, and connectedness. Safety is even more vital in the treatment of trauma survivors who have had experiences of danger, terror, and fragmentation. Safety includes physical, psychological, social, and moral components (Bloom, Foderaro, & Ryan, 2006). It is foundational to the treatment of complex, multi-layered trauma (Courtois, 2014). Winnicott refers to the "holding environment" as the safe space in which healthy development, creativity, and exploration can occur. He suggests that the safety provided by the holding environment does not need to be perfect; it simply has to be "good enough" (Winnicott, 1939-1970; Elliott, 1994). In the context of group treatment, safety can be developed through creation of group rules, cohesion, and a consistent routine.

Group rules

The development of group boundaries is instrumental to the creation of an emotionally safe group. The group boundaries/rules provide context for how group members should interact with one another and how group members will work toward the overall vision. There is no mandatory list of group rules. But there are general principles that should guide the co-creation of these boundaries. Rules should be shaped by members' needs as they seek to successfully participate. They should also be informed by the group leader's needs as they seek to facilitate a successful group. Yalom (1970) adds that group rules should speak to the group's ability to monitor itself, identify boundaries for self-disclosure, develop structures and procedures, show support for one another, and create mechanisms for managing conflict.

Cohesion

Another factor that facilitates group safety is cohesion. Cohesion is to group treatment what the therapeutic relationship is to individual therapy. Cohesion is defined by Yalom (1970) as "feeling at home," the development of an environment in which group members "feel warmth and comfort in the group and a sense of belongingness; they value the group and feel in turn that they are valued, accepted, and supported by other members" (p. 55-56). Cohesion promotes a sense of loyalty, connection, and strength. Yalom states of the benefits of cohesion, "Those with a greater sense of solidarity, or 'we-ness,' value the group more highly and will defend it against internal and external threats. Such groups have a higher rate of attendance, participation, and mutual support" (Yalom, 1970, p. 55).

Group Routine

Regularity and consistency contribute to a group's sense of safety (Winnicott, 1939) . A group routine does not need to be complicated or tedious. The purpose of a routine is to provide a structured framework for the group process. Although the thematic content, emotional reactions, and interpersonal dynamics of a group can be unpredictable at times, a consistent format contributes to the health and consistency of the group. The facilitator can work collaboratively with the group to create structure or the facilitator can independently decide how to organize the group's activities. Some leaders begin group with a "check-in," proceed to group processing, and end with a "check-out." Others begin with psychoeducational content and end with group processing. Some group facilitators integrate creative and/or artistic activities into the group routine. The manner in which the group is structured should be based on the needs of the group while also taking contextual factors into account.

Storiez helps trauma survivors *CREATE*, *VOICE*, and *HONOR* their narratives.

Defining the Role of the Group Facilitator

Practitioners cannot lead groups without their own experiences, leadership styles, theoretical preferences, and perspectives influencing their approach; facilitators bring each of these to the group context. An individual's leadership style impacts the creative and destructive processes taking place from session to session. A group leader's role will undoubtedly be influenced by the theoretical approach that he/she chooses, however, regardless of one's preferred theoretical orientation, the group leader must fulfill several responsibilities. They must adopt an attitude "of concern, acceptance, genuineness, and empathy" even in the face of conflict, contention, and resistance (Yalom, 1970, p. 117). The group leader must attend to the "creation and maintenance of the group, building [of] a group culture, and activation and illumination of the here and now" (Yalom, 1970 p. 118). Further, the facilitator is charged with the unspoken task of answering these two questions: "Can group members trust you?" and "How did you handle stressors" (Kahn & Aronson, 2007, p. 289). Additional responsibilities include acknowledging and tolerating the unpredictability and spontaneity of group (Phillips, 2013) and setting the stage for what is allowed in group and what boundaries will be upheld.

Group leaders must remain attuned to the emotional climate of the group while also tolerating their own "affective immersion in the group's affective pain" (Phillips, 2013, p. 33). The facilitator must process their own emotions while also facilitating the emotional expression of the group (Phillips, 2013). The task of the group leader is complex- holding the group's pain while also enabling it to move through the pain to achieve "reflection and formulation" (Phillips, 2013, p. 33). Management of countertransference – the impact of our interactions with clients/groups on our own thoughts and feelings as practitioners- is also an essential role of the group leader. Countertransference becomes even more complex in the facilitation of groups with trauma survivors. The clinician is charged with the complicated task of creating connection and remaining emotionally available even as the collective impact of the group's experiences simultaneously effects him/her (Phillips, 2013, p. 36). Phillips (2013) describes this experience as "walking into the lion's den to touch and connect with that which is feared" (p. 33).

Some groups are led by individual facilitators and others by co-facilitators. Courtois (2018) suggests that for those groups led by co-facilitators, it is essential for leaders to collaboratively discuss their group approach. This ensures consistency and guards against splitting during group processing.

The STORIEZ process looks DIFFERENT for every group.

Integrating Storiez into the Group Setting

There are two Storiez trauma narrative formats that can be used when supporting an individual or group in telling their story. The underlying principles for both narrative formats are the same- meeting the client where they are, adopting a strengths-based perspective, integrating and organizing memories, containing traumatic experiences, facilitating the creative expression of life experiences, and developing a future vision.

The full trauma narrative process as presented in *Storiez: A Guide for Therapists* (Corrado, 2015) and *Storiez: A Guide for Children and Teenagers* (Corrado, 2015) is intended for implementation by master's level clinicians (or clinicians in training) to use with individuals/groups in the context of therapy. It assists the trauma survivor in creating a fully detailed trauma narrative that explores past positive and negative experiences, organizes those experiences, and identifies a future vision.

The abbreviated trauma narrative process as introduced in *Storiez: A Do It Yourself Guide* (Corrado, 2016) presents information on how to create a trauma narrative outside the context of therapy without a trained clinician. It can be used independently, or a trauma survivor can complete the process with the support of a family member, friend, or community leader. It can also be used by clinicians in settings where the group/individual does not have the time or resources to complete a full trauma narrative. The *Do It Yourself* process is shorter and does not require that the trauma survivor go into as much detail about their experiences, however, it does follow the same principles and general formatting as *Storiez: A Guide for Therapists* (Corrado, 2015).

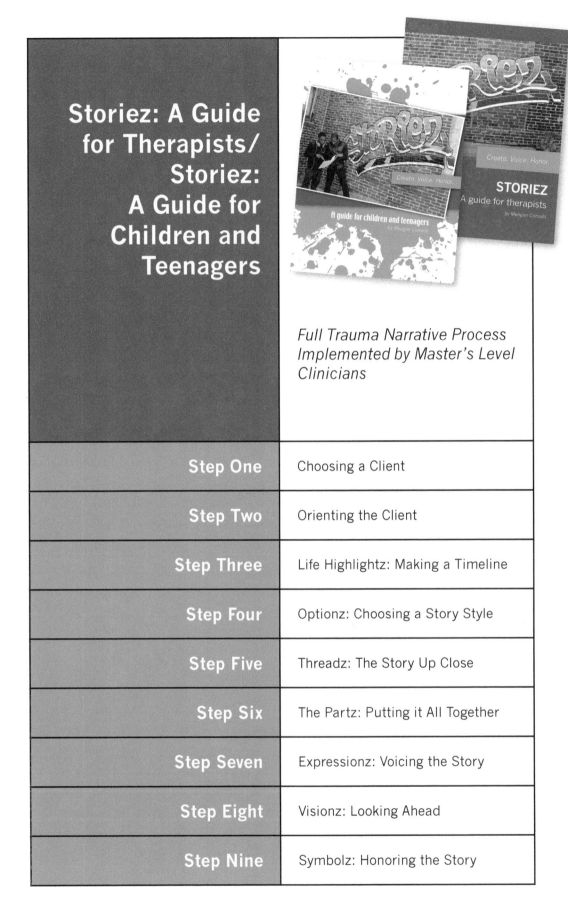

Storiez: A Guide for Therapists/ Storiez: A Guide for Children and Teenagers

Full Trauma Narrative Process Implemented by Master's Level Clinicians

Step One	Choosing a Client
Step Two	Orienting the Client
Step Three	Life Highlightz: Making a Timeline
Step Four	Optionz: Choosing a Story Style
Step Five	Threadz: The Story Up Close
Step Six	The Partz: Putting it All Together
Step Seven	Expressionz: Voicing the Story
Step Eight	Visionz: Looking Ahead
Step Nine	Symbolz: Honoring the Story

Storiez: A Do It Yourself Guide

Abbreviated Trauma Narrative Process Implemented Independently or With the Support of a Clinical or Non-Clinical Support Person

Step One	Supportz
Step Two	Feelingz
Step Three	Lidz: Your Story Box
Step Four	Life Highlightz: Making a Timeline
Step Five	Threadz: Your Story Up Close
Step Six	The Partz: Putting it All Together
Step Seven	Reflectionz: Reviewing Your Story
Step Eight	Visionz: Looking Ahead
Step Nine	Expressionz: Honor Project

Before you decide which version of Storiez to implement in your current group context, consider how much time you have to work with the group, how deeply group members may (or may not) be able to fully process experiences in a group context, consistency in attendance, and demands placed on you/the group from your host setting or funding sources. For an ongoing, consistent therapy group with motivated, engaged members, the full version of Storiez may be appropriate. For time-limited groups or groups that are held in a host setting, the abbreviated version of Storiez may be a better fit.

Once you decide which version of Storiez will be most appropriate for your group, it is important for you to consider how to integrate Storiez into your group routine. Will you begin with a "feelings check-in," have each individual work on their narrative, and then collectively process emotions during a "check out?" Will you begin with psychoeducation about trauma and then support group members in working on their collective story about a shared experience? Your group routine should be customized based on the needs of the group and the opportunities/demands of the setting in which you will be introducing the intervention. Remember, every Storiez session (whether individual or group) looks different for each individual/community.

Provided below are case examples. You will be presented with information about the setting, composition, and needs of the group. You will then find ideas about potential ways to integrate Storiez into the specific group's routine. As you read these scenarios, keep in mind that there is no formula, recipe, or short-cuts for group treatment. These illustrations are tools to support you in thinking through a customized plan for your own groups.

Case Example #1:

A school administrator provides you with a list of 20 children who have experienced grief and loss issues. The list includes names of children who have been through one loss and children who have experienced multiple losses. The children range in age from 7 to 13. The administrator informs you that group sessions should be no longer than 45 minutes and that the group should span about 8 weeks. You have a small room in the school to use for sessions.

You begin by choosing your theoretical model. You then think through issues of group composition. You know that you will have to break this large list into smaller, more manageable groups. You are unsure about how to divide the children because you have never met any of the children on the list. You schedule pre-group interviews and speak to each of the children individually. You gain information about their personality styles, attitude toward group, and traumatic experiences. You talk to them about Storiez. Some of the children are agreeable. Others seem nervous. You assure each of them that they will not be forced to share any part of their story that they are not comfortable sharing and that there will be group rules surrounding confidentiality and respect.

After interviewing each of the children, you begin to assemble the first group, doing your best to create a balance. For this group, you choose two outgoing members, two shy members, a hesitant member, and two individuals whose personalities were difficult to gauge but were enthusiastic to participate.

You then decide on a structure. During pre-group interviews, many of the members mentioned that sometimes it is hard for them to handle their emotions because of the things that they have been through. You decide to make space for this in the group by including a "check in." At the beginning of each session, you encourage group members to express emotions they experienced as a result of their trauma and provide trauma-focused psychoeducation. After the check-in, you then lead the group members through *Storiez: A Do It Yourself Guide* (Corrado, 2016). You choose the abbreviated version of Storiez because you only have 45 minutes each session and the group will only last for 8 weeks. You remember that group members need to be able to reintegrate back into the classroom after sessions are over.

During each group session, you lead the children through a different Storiez step. As they work on their narratives individually, you encourage them to collectively reflect on their thoughts and feelings. At the end of each session, you facilitate a "check-out" activity in which group members identify an emotion they experienced and a healthy way that they can express this emotion outside of group.

Once the group members are nearing the end of their narratives, you talk to them about potential ways that they can honor their stories. The group has bonded and feels safe enough to share their narratives with one another. As their final "Honor Project," they choose to have a candlelight vigil (with battery-operated candles, of course) where each group member shares their story.

Case Example #2:

You are approached by the director of a small outpatient medical practice. One of the employees committed suicide. The practice asks you to help the 10-member office staff process their thoughts and feelings about their collective trauma during a single grief and loss group. A few days before the six-hour group session, you speak to the director to get a better understanding of the office climate, the personalities of the office staff, and their attitude toward group participation. You identify your theoretical model and think through how you can potentially implement Storiez with this group.

As you consider which version of Storiez to implement, you realize that six hours is not enough time for each individual to process their emotions about this trauma and also create individual trauma narratives. Instead, you use Storiez principles and some of the steps to create an adapted Storiez plan. You begin by encouraging group members to identify rules that would be helpful to implement during their day of processing. You acknowledge their collective loss, supporting them as they share their current feelings and experiences about how the trauma has impacted them both personally and professionally. You assist them in identifying sources of strength in the midst of the trauma.

You then introduce an activity to them. You call it the "office story." You set up three different poster boards. They each represent a different phase of the office community's experience. One board is called "where we were." The second is titled "where we are now." The final is named "where we want to be." You explain to the group that they will be working together to identify positive and negative experiences to represent on each poster. You pass out notecards and have group members create positive and negative timeline cards to represent significant events in each phase. They negotiate titles for events and work collaboratively to put the events in sequence. They then create a group vision for how they would like to depict these positive and negative experiences on each poster. The group works collaboratively to create a collage. When their collage is complete, they process their creative experience, acknowledging their collective loss while also discussing their strengths and future vision.

Case Example #3:

You are asked to provide mandatory group therapy to eight youth at a residential treatment program who have a history of chronic victimization. You have no choice regarding which youth are placed in the group, and you know that several of the teenagers do not get along with one another. The group is two hours long and takes place once a week in a private meeting room. Youth will be in the group for two months. Before beginning the group, you choose your theoretical orientation. You conduct pre-group interviews to learn more about the group members and to provide them with an opportunity to discuss their goals and attitude toward participation. Several group members mention trust and confidentiality as a concern for involvement.

During the first group, you assist the members in identifying boundaries/rules for participation. Several express discontent with the fact that the group is mandatory. You decide to allow space for this resistance and give permission for group members to openly express frustrations. During each subsequent session, you attempt to introduce the steps from *Storiez: A Guide for Children and Teenagers*, but you are met with resistance. After several sessions have passed, you directly address the resistance during a group conversation. One group member says, "I'm tired of always having to tell my story." Another says, "People are constantly making us talk about what happened to us." A third adds, "We live here together. If we talk about our stories in group, other people will use what happened against us in an argument." You validate their concerns, acknowledging that their feedback relates to a desire for control over their own stories, a common theme amongst trauma survivors.

You bring a stack of notecards to the next session. You ask group members to write down (or draw) the names of three positive life events and three negative life events. You assure them that they do not have to share these with anyone in the room. You reach into your bag and pull out a few cameras. "We are taking a walk today," you say. "I want you to use these cameras to take photos of things in your environment that express what you felt and thought about the events on your notecards." You traipse around the expansive residential campus together. At various points along the way, group members stop to take photos.

You repeat this process each week until everyone has taken photos to represent each of their life experiences. You print the photos out. The youth place the photos in chronological order. They reflect on their photo story. You ask them to share thoughts, feelings, and experiences as they feel comfortable. The next week, you facilitate another walk. This time, group members are asked to take photos of what they see for themselves in the future. During the final group, each member shares their photos and articulates their future vision.

Case Example #4:

You are charged with the task of creating a Storiez group at an outpatient facility. Your agency has a 6-month waiting list and wants you to provide clients with 3 months of group therapy while they are waiting to be connected to an individual provider. Each group will be an hour and a half long and will take place at the outpatient facility. You schedule a date and time for pre-group interviews. Your clients range in age from 6 to 18 and have diverse experiences· from homelessness and community violence to abuse and neglect. As you review the information from the pre-group interviews, you decide to organize members based on common themes in their experiences. There are 6 children and teenagers who have experienced homelessness. Although they range in age from 7 to 13, you believe that their common experience will unite them.

You begin each session by introducing a coping activity and supporting group members as they practice it. During the second part of the group, you introduce *Storiez: A Guide for Children and Teenagers*. Instead of supporting youth in creating an entire life story, you support them in creating a story surrounding the theme of "home." They create positive and negative notecards based on this theme and select a story style. During each session, they detail their thoughts, feelings, and experiences in the format they have chosen. Some choose to write. Others choose to draw. You end each group session by having individuals share insights about their storytelling experience.

While you are facilitating this group, you are also facilitating other thematic groups. One group's stories center around safety and violence. Another group's theme centers around connection and separation. You implement the same structure for these additional groups.

Case Example #5:

You are in charge of 30 youth participating in an arts-based after school program. The program is situated in a neighborhood notorious for poverty and violence. You have the help of two assistants. Although you have had extensive experience working with at-risk youth, you do not have a social work degree. Despite the fact that you do not have a clinical background, many of the youth talk to you about their traumatic community experiences and even depict these experiences in the artwork that they create.

With the permission of the children's caregivers, you introduce *Storiez: A Do It Yourself Guide* to the youth in your program. You readjust your after school curriculum to devote 30 minutes a day to the storytelling process for a period of two weeks. You divide the class based on personality types and which students are able to interact with the least amount of conflict.

You and your assistants lead the youth through the initial Storiez steps, paying special attention to safety planning and emotional regulation. You encourage the youth to develop a story relating to their experiences living in their neighborhood. They name positive and negative neighborhood experiences. They detail thoughts and feelings about these experiences. They create a future vision for their neighborhood.

You then present three different artistic options for youth to choose for their honor project: painting, mixed media, and mosaic. You and the other leaders divide the children into groups based on their preferred medium and support them in creating an honor project. As they create, you facilitate discussion amongst them about their thoughts, feelings, experiences, and artistic process. When the youth complete their Storiez, you facilitate a Storiez exhibition in which those who are comfortable share their Honor Projects.

Caregiver Permission Letter

Date _____

Dear _____,

My name is_____. I am contacting you from _____. I am writing to request your permission to allow _____ to participate in Storiez. Storiez helps children, teenagers, and adults look back at past positive and negative experiences, organize them, and develop a future vision. If given your permission, your child will create his/her own story with the assistance of_____. This will take place from _____. Thank you for your consideration. Please contact me with any questions.

Sincerely,

_____

Conclusion

At first sight, group treatment can feel intimidating. Daunting. But it doesn't have to. While it is true that group treatment involves bringing together a diverse collection of individuals, each with different challenges, strengths, and personalities, the group setting is also bubbling with potential for transformation and growth. There will be chaos, conflict, and resistance in the groups that you facilitate. Every group will not be comfortable or smooth. Some will test the boundaries of your own emotional capacity. But hidden in the chaotic, stormy moments of the groups you facilitate, there is strength, creativity, and transformation. As you seek to integrate Storiez into your group routine, remember these important points:

- Groups contain the potential for both destruction and creativity. Honor and make space for the chaos. It will ultimately lead to creativity, progress, and growth.

- Group composition is not a science; it is an art. Given the strengths/limitations of the individuals in your group and the benefits/constraints of your setting, do the best you can to create balance.

- You do not have to be a perfect group facilitator to lead a successful group. Do the best that you can with the resources that you have to provide a meaningful group experience for participants.

- Safety is an essential component of any healthy group and includes multiple domains. Within the context of a safe environment, a group can successfully achieve its goals. Without safety, a group is unable to achieve the fullness of its potential.

- Every Storiez process is different. Allow Storiez to meet the needs of your group rather than forcing the group to conform to your Storiez agenda.

- How can you implement Storiez in a group context? Allow the needs of the individuals/groups to whom you are providing treatment to shape and mold their own unique Storiez process.

Appendix: Group Plan

Group Name: _____ Group Dates:_____

Strength and Resiliency Factors

Shared experiences		Institutional support		Respect for group boundaries		Pre-group interviews	
Creativity		Motivation		Cohesion		Expressivity	
Reflectivity		Adaptability		Openness		Empathy	

Barriers

Aggression		Avoidance		Boundary challenges		Denial	
Institutional resistance		Chaotic environment		Inconsistent engagement		Confidentiality challenges	

Structure

Open		Voluntary		Time limited	
Closed		Involuntary		Ongoing	

Purpose

Self-help		Support		Psychoeducation	
Therapeutic		Process		Other:	

Composition

Age range	Trauma types	Size

Agency

Time Frame

Authorization Period		Session Frequency	

Context

Outpatient		In-Home		Community		Hospital	
Residential		School		Shelter		Other:	

Group Plan:

Is the group ready for Storiez? Why/why not? If not, when might it be ready?

Are there issues that the group should work on prior to introduction of Storiez?

How can I incorporate Storiez into the existing group process?

How detailed can group members' stories be based on the limitations of my setting?

How would I introduce Storiez to the group?

Bibliography

Bloom, S., Foderaro, J., & Ryan, R. (2006). *A trauma-informed psychoeducational group curriculum*. Philadelphia: Community Works.

Bonebright, D. (2010). 40 years of storming: a historical review of Tuckman's model of small group development. *Human Resource Development International*, 13, 111-120.

Brabender, V., Fallon, A., & Smolar, A. (2004). *Essentials of group therapy*. Hoboken: John Wiley & Sons.

Briere, J. & Scott, C. (2006). *Principles of trauma therapy: a guide to symptoms, evaluation, and treatment*. Sage: Thousand Oaks.

Chapman, L., Morabito, D., Ladakakos, C., Schreier, H., & Knudson, M. (2001). The effectiveness of art therapy interventions in reducing post traumatic stress disorder symptoms in pediatric patients. *Art Therapy*, 18, 100-104.

Classen, C., Cavanaugh, C., Kaupp, J., Aggarwal, R., Palesh, O., Koopman, C.,... Spiegel, D. (2011). A comparison of trauma-focused and present-focused group therapy for survivors of childhood sexual abuse: a randomized controlled trial. *Psychological Trauma: Theory, Research, Practice, and Policy*, 3, 84-93.

Corrado, M. (2015). *Storiez: a guide for children and teenagers*. Philadelphia: Ingram Spark.

Corrado, M. (2015). *Storiez: a guide for therapists*. Philadelphia: Ingram Spark.

Corrado, M. (2016). *Storiez: a do it yourself guide*. Philadelphia: Ingram Spark.

Corrado, M. (2016). *Trauma narratives with inner city youth: the Storiez intervention*. (Doctoral dissertation). Retrieved from https://repository.upenn.edu/edissertations_sp2/77/.

Courtois, C. (2014) Complex traumatic stress disorders: advances in conceptualization and evidence-based treatment [Powerpoint slides]. Retrieved October 17, 2014.

Courtois, C. (2018). *Untitled*. Personal Collection of Dr. Christine Courtois, Consulting and Training in Trauma Psychology and Treatment, Bethany Beach, DE.

Dokter, D. (2010). Helping and hindering processes in creative arts therapy group practice. *Group*, 34, 67-83.

Elliott, Diana. Impaired object relations in professional women molested as children. (1994). *Psychotherapy*, 31, 79-86.

Erikson, E. (1994). *Identity and the life cycle*. New York: W.W. Norton.

Haen, C. & Weil, M. (2010). Group therapy on the edge: adolescence, creativity, and group work. *Creative Arts Therapy*, 34, 37-52.

Hardiman, G. & Zernich, T. (1980). Some considerations of Piaget's cognitive-structuralist theory and children's artistic development. *Studies in Art Education*, 21, 12-19.

Hurster, T. (2009). *Group treatment*. Personal Collection of Thomas Hurtser, Bryn Mawr College, Bryn Mawr, PA.

Johnson, D. (1987). The role of creative arts therapies in the diagnosis and treatment of psychological trauma. *The Arts in Psychotherapy*, 14, 7-13.

Kahn, G. & Aronson, S. (2007). Group treatment for traumatized adolescents: special considerations. *Trauma and Group Therapy*, 31, 281-292.

Lauer, R. & Goldfield, M. (1970). Creative writing in group therapy. *Psychotherapy: Theory, Research, and Practice*, 7, 248-252.

Layne, C., Saltzman, W., Savjak, N., Popovic, T., Music, M., Djapo, N.,...Houston, R. (2001). Trauma/grief focused group psychotherapy: school-based postwar intervention with traumatized Bosnian adolescents. *Group Dynamics: Theory, Research, and Practice*, 5, 277-290.

McMullen, J., O'Callaghan, P., Shannon, C., Black, A., & Eakin, J. (2013). Group trauma-focused cognitive behavioural therapy with former child soldiers and other war-affected boys in the DR Congo: a randomized controlled trial. The Journal of Child Psychology and Psychiatry, 54, 1231-1241.

Meeks, J. (1971). *The fragile alliance: an orientation to the outpatient psychotherapy of adolescents*. Baltimore: Williams & Wilkins.

Miller, C., Eisner, W., & Allport, C. (1994). Creative coping: a cognitive behavioral group for borderline personality disorder. *Archives of Psychiatric Nursing*, 8, 280-285.

Nitsun, M. (1996). *The anti-group: destructive forces in the group and their creative potential*. London: Routledge.

Phillips, S. (2013). From immersion to formulation and integration. *Group*, 37, 31-39.

Reineke, M. (2007). Creativity, destruction, and mimesis in Winnicott and Girard. *Contagion: Journal of Violence, Mimesis, and Culture*, 14, 79-95.

Rutan, J., Stone, W., & Shay, J. (2007). *Psychodynamic group psychotherapy*. New York: Guilford Press.

Salloum, A., Garside, L., Irwin, C., Anderson, A., & Francois, A. (2009). Grief and trauma group therapy for children after Hurricane Katrina. *Social Work with Groups*, 32, 64-79.

Saltzman, W., Layne, C., Pynoos, R., Steinberg, A., & Aisenberg, E. (2001). Trauma and grief-focused intervention for adolescents exposed to community violence: results of school-based screening and group treatment protocol. *Group Dynamics: Theory, Research, and Practice*, 5, 291-303.

Stewart, D. & Thomson, K. (2005). The face your fear club: therapeutic group work with young children as a response to community trauma in northern Ireland. *The British Journal of Social Work*, 35, 104-124.

Tuckman, B. (1965). Developmental sequence in small groups. *Psychological Bulletin*, 63, 384-399.

Van der Kolk, B. (1987). The role of the group in the origin and resolution of the trauma response. In Van der Kolk (Ed.), *Psychological Trauma*. Washington DC: American Psychiatric Press.

Winnicott, D.W. (1939-1970). *Deprivation and delinquency*. London: Lavistock.

Winnicott, D.W. (2005). *Playing and reality*. London: Routledge.

Yalom, I. (1970). *The theory and practice of group psychotherapy*. New York: Basic Books.

About the Author

Meagan Corrado is a Doctor of Social Work and a Licensed Clinical Social Worker. She is the creator of the Storiez Trauma Narrative intervention and has authored seven books. She provides therapy to inner city youth in the Philadelphia and Camden, NJ areas. She earned her Doctorate of Social Work from the University of Pennsylvania in 2016, her Masters of Social Services from Bryn Mawr College in 2009, and her Bachelors of Social Work from Cairn University in 2008. She specializes in work with children and teenagers who have had difficult life experiences. She completed trainings in a variety of modalities. Her experience includes clinical work in a variety of settings including community mental health agencies, residential treatment facilities, schools, hospitals, and homes. She takes a creative approach to her work with children, adolescents, and families, incorporating elements of art, music, poetry, and play therapy in her clinical practice. Dr. Meagan's interest in helping others process difficult life experiences began at a very early age when she helped family members and friends process feelings about significant life issues. Storiez stems from Dr. Meagan's own personal experiences with trauma, as well as her clinical work with children, adolescents, and families.

Additional Resources

Storiez Trauma Narratives offers engaging resources, interactive training, and community engagement opportunities to young survivors of trauma and their service providers with the goal of helping youth creatively express past experiences, actively use their voices as a vehicle for change, and honor the strength and resilience within their narratives.

Check out these additional Storiez resources:

Storiez: A Guide for Therapists

Storiez: A Guide for Children and Teenagers

Storiez: A DIY Guide

Storiez: A Feelingz Guide

You Are Never Lost

Stronger Than You Think

CPSIA information can be obtained
at www.ICGtesting.com
Printed in the USA
BVHW020202160820
586532BV00004B/82